It's all about the ...

Reboot, Reinvent, & Restore your life

By Pastor Bill Jenkins

It's all about the…

RESET

Reboot, Reinvent & Restore Your Life

By Pastor Bill Jenkins

All scripture quotations in this book are taken from the King James Version of the Bible unless otherwise noted

Copyright © 2017
All Rights Reserved

Published by:
Church of ACTS
3740 S. Dearborn St.
Indianapolis, IN 46237

Table of Contents

Introduction 1

Chapter 1
RESET Signs 7

Chapter 2
RESET Means 13

Chapter 3
RESET Involves 17

Chapter 4
RESET Acronym 25

Chapter 5
RESET Your Mindset 33

Chapter 6
RESET Your Life 39

Chapter 7
RESET 30-Day Devotional 45

Chapter 8
RESET Scriptures 79

Conclusion 85

INTRODUCTION

If you're in a slump, feel burned out in life, or if things haven't been going your way for an extended period of time, you might want to consider a RESET!! The word Reset means to set again or set anew. It means to set something back to its original condition and state. It's used in reference to putting something back to its original position, such as a broken bone or a mileage odometer.

Sometimes in life, through our bad choices or other people imposing their will on us, we can get off course and stray from God's original plan. It's important to realize this as fast as we can to avoid digging a deeper hole that will only require more time to get out of later in life. It's then we need to allow God to Reset our lives and get us back on the right road!

> *"But ye have not so learned Christ: If so be that ye have heard him, and have been taught by him, as the truth is in Jesus: That ye put off concerning the former conversation the old*

man, which is corrupt according to the deceitful lusts; And be renewed in the spirit of your mind; And that ye put on the new man, which after God is created in righteousness and true holiness." Ephesians 4:20-24

Resetting your life doesn't mean you go to the extreme by divorcing your spouse, quitting your job, leaving your church, or moving out of state. It could be a simple tweak that might make a world of difference.

Hitting the Reset button is about five things:

1. **Realizing you are off course**
   The key to getting on course is discovering that you have been off course.

2. **Repenting of your sins of commission and omission**

   Sins of commission = sins that you are intentionally and knowingly doing that need to stop.

Sins of omission = things that you are neglecting or leaving out of your daily routine that you need to incorporate into your life.

3. **Relinquishing your will to God's will alone**
   The important thing to remember about relinquishing your will is not just allowing God to take over, but being quiet during the process.

4. **Refining the vision**
   Refining the vision doesn't mean changing the vision it means clarifying the vision.

5. **Refiring the engine**
   Refiring is about getting things going again in the right direction in your life.

Once you realize you're off course, it's important not to start blaming others for your lack of progress. Always look inwardly first, and draw a circle around yourself. Ask yourself, "What needs to start again in my life?" and "What am I doing that needs to stop?" After seeking those answers, let go of your will and

desires while yielding yourself to God. Jesus set the perfect example for all of us as Christians to follow.

"For I came down from heaven, not to do mine own will, but the will of him that sent me." John 6:38

"And he said, Abba, Father, all things are possible unto thee; take away this cup from me: nevertheless not what I will, but what thou wilt." Mark 14:36

"Jesus saith unto them, My meat is to do the will of him that sent me, and to finish his work." John 4:34

After we allow the Lord to truly take back charge of our lives, it's then God can refine the vision and give you back godly purpose for your future. All that's left for you to do is refire up the spiritual engine, and let Jesus take the wheel. It sounds easy, but I know it can be difficult. That's why I wrote this book, to help be a spiritual GPS and navigate you into a successful future. Anything worth having will take work to obtain and maintain. So never be afraid to put your

---

hand to the plow, and work hard to get your victory in Jesus Name.

If you are sensing burnout or staleness in your life, and feel like you're stuck in a rut, then allow the words of the Holy Spirit to be like a tow truck and help pull you out of the ditch. It is past time you allow the Lord to put your mileage odometer back to zero and give you a fresh start. Now is the time to get those broken bones Reset, so you can be at full strength to overcome the enemy and be whole in your life. Come on! Let's hit the Reset Button together!!

Chapter 1

Six Signs you Need a RESET

Sometimes you can reboot a computer; other times you need to Reset the computer. A reboot is temporary, where as a Reset is more permanent. A reboot is when you hold down the power button and turn off the device. The hope is that when you turn it back on, it functions in a brand new way and the "bugs" have been worked out. A Reset is when you take the device back to its original factory settings. At this crucial hour in the history of mankind, we need more than a "reboot"; we need a "Reset."

It's important as Christians to discern when you need a Reset in your life. Below are some characteristics that people experience when they are burned out. This list will help you determine if you need a Reset.

Characteristics of Burnout

- Weariness
- Lack of vision
- Complaining
- Dissatisfaction

- Low energy
- Discouragement
- Easily aggravated
- Health issues
- Stressed out
- Staleness in relationship with God
- Decrease in passion
- Procrastination
- No creativity
- Loss of Joy
- Lack of production/fruit

Obviously those attributes are things that all of us face on a daily basis, however if enough of the symptoms are reoccurring, then you might need to self-diagnose that it is time to begin to Reset your life.

Reset Signs

1. **When you are finding wrong and wrong is finding you**
   Sometimes we all make mistakes in our efforts to achieve success in life, but other times wrong has a way of just finding you. Bad things, contaminated things, and negative things seem to be drawn to you like a magnet.

It begins to affect your ability to put a positive spin on life any longer. Where you used to be able to use the negative to your advantage, it's now becoming too blinding for you to see the good.

2. **When you are focused on what you "have to" do instead of what you "get to" do**
Burnout often is revealed when we can't appreciate obstacles as opportunities. We become inconvenienced and burdened by work. Some think work is a curse. Others think work is a way to invest time in order to make a difference. Your perspective is key in understanding whether you're burned out or fired up.

3. **When you have a victim's mentality**
Constantly viewing yourself as a victim does not empower you to change your present circumstances. The problem with seeing yourself as a victim is that it gives you permission to remain in a rut. You will use it as an excuse to never move into your future. Yes,

there are really bad people who have done really bad things to some really good people. Yes, there are those who have experienced more unfortunate circumstances than others, however, it is God's will for you to be the victor in all things. Allow the Lord to turn around your bad situations for a good use in the world.

4. **When you feel you have untapped potential**
It's always important to have high expectations and realistic ambitions as part of your life. We always want to be balanced and never go overboard in making unreasonable goals for your future. However, when there is more to you than you're being allowed to discover, and you're being held back from fulfilling your dreams, it could mean it's time to Reset.

5. **When you no longer celebrate victories**
The hardships of today are the price you pay for the successes of tomorrow. Victories are to be relished and celebrated. When you can't celebrate a victory for fear it's just another

failure in disguise waiting to appear, you are definitely experiencing burnout. You can't just mourn the failures but forget to celebrate the victories and then believe everything is okay.

6. **When anger consumes your life and defines who you are**

    Discouragement leads to anger, and continual discouragement leads to greater anger. If you are constantly disagreeing with those to whom you would normally not disagree with, then that is a sign you're not dealing with things in a proper way in your own heart. If the road rage is going up, and the patience level is going down, you need more than a tune-up. You need a Reset.

You are not a bad person if you need to Reset your life. It may just mean you stayed in one season of your life too long. It could also mean you have outgrown your usefulness in one stage, and you're ready for another. It might be as simple as you need to readjust your priorities, and place your focus back on what is truly important in life.

"For precept must be upon precept, precept upon precept; line upon line, line upon line; here a little, and there a little:

For with stammering lips and another tongue will he speak to this people.

To whom he said, This is the rest wherewith ye may cause the weary to rest; and this is the refreshing: yet they would not hear.

But the word of the Lord was unto them precept upon precept, precept upon precept; line upon line, line upon line; here a little, and there a little; that they might go, and fall backward, and be broken, and snared, and taken."
Isaiah 28:10-13

Chapter 2

What Does RESET Mean?

Resetting your life might involve some initial pain and suffering. You could lose some sleep at night. Resetting could also mean a loss of income. You might even feel isolated and rejected by others, but ultimately, you must trust that resetting your life will yield far greater results and rewards than choosing to stay on a path that is heading nowhere.

Reset Means:

1. **You are needing a break**
   You have to step back from the chaos of life and clear your head. You have to have some down time and give yourself permission to relax and rejuvenate your spirit. Put the phone away, shut the radio and TV off, and minimize the time on social media. Just allow the Lord to be the sole source of beginning the Reset.

2. You are looking for alternative means to complete a task

Burnout often begins when you hit a wall where nothing is working and you are out of ideas. It's then you get to the point where you look for alternative ways to complete the job. Some of those ways may have never been tried before. God may be calling you to go down an untrailed path and leave a smoking trail for others to follow. You have to think outside of the box, and go to the next-level of thinking. This scares some people and keeps them from achieving great success. Be willing to do different things, if you want to see different results.

3. You are needing a fresh perspective

You lose your joy when things became stale. Reading a book, asking an expert a question, going to a seminar, and spending time with the Lord are all ways to freshen up your perspective. Your perspective in life determines your prosperity. Are you a half-empty or a half-full person? Magnifying the

right things can help make you a more positive person. When you use a magnifying glass, an object doesn't get bigger; it's just your perception of the object that gets bigger. Magnifying the Lord will help you to keep your perspective fresh in your life.

4. You are stuck in a rut
Usually when your car gets stuck in mud or snow, you're going to need help to get out of the mess. Pastors, spouses, coaches, counselors, and accountability partners are great people to go to when needing help to get unstuck in life. Being stuck is like being in a slump. Every person needs spiritual leadership to help give them guidance in times of trouble.

5. You are ready for change
Life can throw you an unexpected curve ball that can change the course and direction of your life. Personal sickness, death in the family, job loss, and divorce are things that happen in life that can require a major adjustment moving forward. Sometimes it just

may be a desire for something different. Life happens in seasons.

> *"To every thing there is a season, and a time to every purpose under the heaven:"*
> Ecclesiastes 3:1

What worked in one season may not work in the next season. We must be willing to accept change and adjust to different things in life. If you are in need of a Reset and want to know where to begin, here are four questions to ask yourself:

1. What is the change I want to make?
2. Why do I want to make a change?
3. What is stopping me from making the change?
4. How am I going to make the change?

Make sure you know what the Reset means, so you can determine if you're ready to hit the Reset button for your life.

Chapter 3

What Hitting the RESET Involves

One of the keys to spiritual success is doing what you can do and leaving the rest for the Lord to do. God will not do your job, and doesn't want you to do His job either. When you cooperate with the Lord, you are going to put yourself in the best position to succeed in life. The goal of this personal cooperation with the Lord is threefold:

1. To live victoriously
2. To promote unity
3. To extend the kingdom of God

You will never go wrong when you involve the Lord in your life and cooperate with Him to obtain success.

Reset Involves:

1. **Letting go of your past and looking forward into your future**

   Never allow your past to dictate your future. Never allow the enemy to convince you there is something to go back to in your past. One

thing that helps me, and may help you, is to always remember Lot's wife.

"As a dog returneth to his vomit, so a fool returneth to his folly." Proverbs 26:11

2. Turning your stumbling blocks into stepping stones

Obstacles should be viewed through the lens of opportunity. Don't let obstacles be a setback. Let them be a setup for God to reveal His glory to you in your life. God not only doesn't want you to waste your pain, but He doesn't want grief to hold you back from using difficult situations to help others. You must be aware of the stages of grief and evaluate if you are letting it hold you back.

The 5 Stages of Grief

1. Depression
2. Denial
3. Bargaining
4. Anger
5. Acceptance

Resetting is about accepting who you are and what you have gone through up until this point in your life. You don't have to have liked it, or believe that everything was a part of God's perfect plan, but it is what it is. You have to allow God to turn things around for your advantage, even in the worst of circumstances. Whether it was a personal bad decision, or a decision imposed upon you by someone else, you have to accept the things you cannot change, and turn them into stepping stones.

3. Establishing a good first-fruit foundation

It's more important than ever to establish a good first-fruit foundation. Whatever you do with the first part and portion, determines what happens with the rest. It's important to do the right thing with the first part of your money, day, year, and relationships, so the rest can be blessed.

4. Evaluating WHO is in your circle

"Be not deceived: evil communications corrupt good manners." 1 Corinthians 15:33

It's essential to your spiritual health that you are connected to people who are going to help you and not hurt you. We need others to make us better and not bitter. From time to time, evaluate your friendship to make sure they are adding value and not draining your tank of joy. Every relationship must be mutually beneficial or it won't last.

5. Chasing Life

Get rid of dead things in your life. The first thing Noah did when the Ark landed on the mountain was send a dove to find life.

4 Things that Living Things do:
- Eat
- Grow
- Detox – get rid of waste
- Reproduce

If you are alive, these four things will be a part of your life. However, it is not just about living life, it is about chasing life!

"Thou wilt shew me the path of life: in thy presence is fulness of joy; at thy right hand there are pleasures for evermore." Psalm 16:11

"Now the God of hope fill you with all joy and peace in believing, that ye may abound in hope, through the power of the Holy Ghost." Romans 15:13

5 Ways to Chase Life:

- Pursue the Author of Life - God
- Laugh more
- Do more fun things
- Make a bucket list and start knocking things off the list
- Do something for the first time

When is the last time you did something for the first time?

6. **Rejoicing in your life**

   It's time to rejoice! You have made it through some stuff that was intended to kill you. You have endured some storms that were designed by the enemy to take you out. Rejoice because you are alive and God's not done with you yet.

   Rejoice = Re – Joy or enjoy again

   Resetting is about giving you the ability to enjoy life again.

7. **Being willing to change and make all necessary corrections to improve your current condition**

   Your present condition exists and persists with your permission. If there are things that you need to change, you can't continue to do the same things, and expect a different result. You must be intentional, premeditated, and determined concerning your Godly behavior.

8. Preparing yourself mentally

If you are going to Reset, you can't be unprepared or underprepared in your mindset.

Unprepared = no preparation
Underprepared = not enough preparation

Preparation is perspiration. It is work. If you are not willing to pay the price and cooperate with God, than why should the Lord work on your behalf?

Resetting is Rethinking. Scientists tell us that we have approximately 60,000 thoughts per day with about 80% being old, regurgitated, or negative thoughts. That's about 47,000 bad or old thoughts. We cannot Reset our minds if we are not thinking anything new or challenging ourselves to go beyond the norm.

9. Not filling in the blanks of life

Resetting is allowing God to fill in the blanks for your future. Sometimes when I hesitate in my conversations with others, they attempt to

finish what I'm trying to say. Most of the time they are mistaken and it causes me to forget what I was going to say. If you are going to have a permanent Reset in your life, you cannot get ahead of God and attempt to out think Him. Allow God to fill in the blanks in your life.

> *"For my thoughts are not your thoughts, neither are your ways my ways, saith the Lord."* Isaiah 55:8

It's not that you don't know what Reset means; it's just that you don't know what Reset will bring. So, trust the Lord that He has your best interest in mind.

Chapter 4

Acronym for RESET

R = Renew

Resetting is renewing. To renew is to make something new, strong, and fresh again.

Renewing Includes:
1. Repairing damage
2. Replacing the old for the new
3. Restoring the freshness

A Reset requires fixing any previous damage, and learning to walk in total forgiveness. It also requires you to go back to your last act of disobedience, and make the wrongs of life right again. You have to replace the old mindsets, with new godly mindsets, in order for the Reset to truly have a lasting impact. When those things are done, a refreshing will be released.

One of the hardest parts of Resetting is ending something old and beginning something new. It might feel like a room without an opening to escape. No windows, no doors, but in reality, there is a way out, and you hold the key. Don't let the fear of not knowing what's on the other side keep you from entering.

> *"And no man putteth new wine into old bottles: else the new wine doth burst the bottles, and the wine is spilled, and the bottles will be marred: but new wine must be put into new bottles." Mark 2:22*

E = Eager

Personal Resets must be accompanied by a desire for self-improvement. You may be good at pointing out the flaws of others, but Resets begin with an enthusiastic hunger to draw a circle around yourself and seek change. To understand what I mean by eagerness, it might be good to understand the opposite of eagerness. The opposite of eagerness is apathy. Apathy is when you lose feeling or stop caring.

It's when you lose interest and become numb to the things in life. That is a dangerous place to land in life, and that's why a Reset is required to generate a passion to reach for the best God offers you.

"Delight thyself also in the LORD: and he shall give thee the desires of thine heart."
Psalm 37:4

S = Surrender

You cannot fully Reset any area of your life until you surrender every area in your life to the Lord. We make Jesus our Savior, but we forget to make Him our Lord. Until you make Jesus Lord *of all* He is not Lord *at all*. The word "Lord" is used in terms of someone ruling or owning something. Does your relationship with Jesus Christ mean He owns and rules your thoughts, your actions, and your life? Are you fully surrendered to the Lord Jesus Christ in every area of your life?

To surrender means to agree to stop fighting, hiding, and resisting because you know that you will not win or succeed without giving up. You internally come to terms with the fact that you have to let go and let God be in charge. You may say Jesus is Lord over your life, but feel the need to give God your two-cents. Don't be a back seat driver who desires to be a co-pilot. Remember that God doesn't need you to be His GPS for your life.

"I beseech you therefore, brethren, by the mercies of God, that ye present your bodies a living sacrifice, holy, acceptable unto God, which is your reasonable service.² And be not conformed to this world: but be ye transformed by the renewing of your mind, that ye may prove what is that good, and acceptable, and perfect, will of God."
Romans 12:1-2

E = Ending

Resetting begins with stopping bad behavior. Reset is really **Releasing Everything So**

Elevation Takes place in your life. You have to end bad behavior, bad relationships, and bad things that desire to keep you from fulfilling your God-given destiny. The Bible encourages you to not be unequally yoked with others in life.

> *"Be ye not unequally yoked together with unbelievers: for what fellowship hath righteousness with unrighteousness? And what communion hath light with darkness?"* 2 Corinthians 6:14

Five Areas Never to be Unequally Yoked In:

- Business
- Marriage
- Government
- Friendships
- Finances

Being unequally yoked will always take you where you don't want to go, cost you more that you can afford to pay, and keep you there longer than you want to stay.

T = Trust

> *"And they that know thy name will put their trust in thee: for thou, LORD, hast not forsaken them that seek thee."* Psalm 9:10

Trust is a belief that someone or something is reliable, good, honest, and effective in all their ways. The opposite of trust is strife. So when there is the presence of trust, there will be the absence of strife. Whenever there is a presence of strife, it's because there is an absence of trust. Resetting is getting to the point where you quit having internal struggles, and stop arguing with God. Resetting is settling the fact that God knows and will always do well by His children. Knowing the nature of God is knowing the characteristics of God. It is knowing He will be there always and will never forsake you. There are a lot of people in the world, and in the church, who have "daddy issues" because of their natural, earthly fathers not meeting their expectations. Don't ever make the mistake of comparing your Heavenly Father with your earthly father. Your Heavenly Father will never let you down.

> *"Oh Lord of hosts, blessed is the man that trusteth in thee."* Psalm 84:12

Resetting isn't always easy, but it's required to stay on course when things aren't working well in your life. Always look inwardly to what you can do instead of pointing fingers and placing blame on others. Remember, you can't control others, you can only control yourself. You don't have to answer for others; you only have to answer for yourself. Take responsibility, do what needs to be done to stay on track, and complete the course of your life faithfully unto the Lord.

"I have fought a good fight, I have finished my course, I have kept the faith:" 2 Timothy 4:7

Chapter 5

RESET your Mindset

Your mind is the single most effective thing the enemy uses to control your life. I've often said, "Sow a thought, reap an action; sow an action, reap a habit; sow a habit, reap a character; sow a character, reap a destiny." In other words, your thoughts determine your destiny. Whatever you think on will ultimately affect your life either in a positive way or a negative way.

> *"A good man out of the good treasure of his heart bringeth forth that which is good; and an evil man out of the evil treasure of his heart bringeth forth that which is evil: for of the abundance of the heart his mouth speaketh."*
> Luke 6:45

If you truly want to Reset your mindset, you have to be militant about controlling your thoughts. Paul says in 2 Corinthians 10:5, that you must *"take into*

captivity every thought to the obedience of Christ." Whatever you don't control in your mind has the potential to control you. Paul also told the Philippian church exactly what they needed to think on to ensure a successful destiny.

> *"Finally, brethren, whatsoever things are true, whatsoever things are honest, whatsoever things are just, whatsoever things are pure, whatsoever things are lovely, whatsoever things are of good report; if there be any virtue, and if there be any praise, think on these things."* Philippians 4:8

8 Things to Dwell on Daily

1. **True** = Think on genuine and authentic truths found in the Word of God; reject anything inconsistent with the Bible.
2. **Honest** = Do not think on illegitimate, dishonest, or deceitful things.
3. **Just** = Think reasonably and lawfully.
4. **Pure** = Impure thoughts weaken and pollute the mind.

5. **Lovely** = Think on beautiful and attractive characteristics in you, others and God.
6. **Good Report** = Only good news and good testimonies should be allowed in your mind.
7. **Virtuous** = Think about how many good and moral things you can do to make a positive difference in others' lives.
8. **Praiseworthy** = If you don't have anything nice to say about God, then shut up your mind and mouth about the devil.

It is so important to remember that the Word of God is always the deciding factor in determining whether or not you are thinking on things that will benefit you. So when you have a thought, just ask yourself WWJD or What Would Jesus Do? But also judge your thoughts against the Scripture. If your thoughts are consumed with negative things that are depressing, or if impure thoughts are leading you away from Christ, then you need to do a better job of being conscious in your mindset so you can control your thoughts. This takes work. If you want to Reset your mindset, you have to fight for it using the Word of God as your weapon.

A wrong mindset is a stronghold for the enemy. Strongholds are mindsets impregnated with hopelessness. The enemy wants to plant hopelessness in your mind concerning your health, your future, your family, your dreams, and your destiny. The devil knows that whatever you believe in your mind, whether it's true or not, will affect your life. You have to force yourself to believe what God thinks and says about you, and not what you believe and think about yourself. You have to train your mind from thinking certain thoughts that are against God's will for your life. Do not allow them to continue. You have to use discipline to replace the negative thoughts with the positive words from Scripture. It won't be easy at first, but you must be willing to fight for your freedom. God will not Reset your mindset; you have to do it yourself with His help.

Once you make the decision to Reset your mindset and start to take authority over your thoughts, there are some practical things you can do to maintain your victory and continue to be an overcomer.

Practical Recipe for Victory

- Get enough sleep
- Meditate on the Word of God
- Declutter your life
- Eat healthy
- Have an accountability partner
- Pray
- Prophesy over yourself
- Avoid evil music and television
- Put on the Armor of God daily
- Read a godly book

These are just a few ways to keep your mind focused on the Lord so you can think the right thoughts. You do your job, and I'm sure the Lord will do His. Together you can Reset your mindset.

Chapter 6

RESET your Life

Resetting your life is like detoxing your soul, or setting your computer back to factory default. There are six main areas to evaluate in considering whether or not you need a Reset.

The Wheel of Life

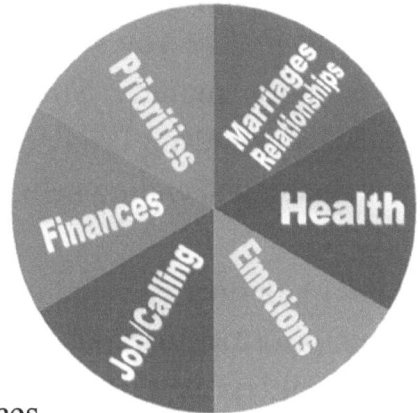

1. Finances
2. Priorities
3. Marriage/relationships
4. Health
5. Emotions
6. Job/Calling

These six areas are usually what end up determining the quality of your life. To whatever level you are experiencing success in each of these areas is the level you will feel satisfied in life.

1. **Reset your Finances**

    If you are in debt, you need to Reset your finances. If you don't have a budget, you need to Reset your finances. Begin a process of getting out of debt by creating a budget, so you know what's coming in and what's going out. You may also realize you need to spend less, and make more money. Stress concerning finances is a bondage you can break by properly managing spending habits.

2. **Reset your Priorities**

    When your priorities are out of order in life you will definitely experience chaos. Here is the proper way to prioritize your life:
    1. God
    2. Family
    3. Job
    4. Church

This is just a short list of how to properly prioritize your life to avoid trouble and define a successful plan.

3. **Reset your Marriage**
Even when God calls people together in holy matrimony, it still takes work for the relationship to succeed. Dating your spouse is crucial to keeping your marriage fresh. There will be times you will have to be mature and come together to redefine expectations and boundaries. Resetting your marriage, or any relationship, doesn't mean it's unsuccessful. It means you are taking responsibility and staying ahead of the curves of life to avoid trouble.

4. **Reset your Health**
Stress, unhealthy eating habits, lack of exercise, and excessive weight gain are all symptoms that could lead you to make a decision to Reset your health.

5. Reset your Emotions

If your negative emotions are controlling your life to the point it is having a negative effect on your daily living, then you need to Reset your emotions. Anger, sadness, depression, worry, jealousy, and grief are things that can be controlled instead of them controlling you. You may need to hit the Reset button with your emotions every day, or even several times a day, depending on the circumstances of life.

6. Reset your Job/Calling

This is the hardest Reset to embark upon because it requires a greater risk and the decision could negatively affect others, not just you.

On all issues of Resetting, it is important to receive wise, godly counsel before spontaneously acting and creating an even greater problem.

Wise Counsel Gives You:

- A second opinion, Proverbs 12:15
- Safety, Proverbs 11:14

- Confirmation, Proverbs 15:22
- Abundant life, Proverbs 4:13
- Peace, Proverbs 24:6

The Bible says wisdom is the principal thing, or the main thing, in life that will release the prosperity of the Lord. Don't try and do a Resetting by yourself. Always seek counsel, and apply godly wisdom to your life to ensure success.

Chapter 7

30-Day RESET Devotional

This devotional will be a little different than most devotionals. I am going to give you a scripture for the day, a thought for the day, a prayer for the day, a place to journal about the day, and a deed for the day. I'm not going to fill pages with a bunch of words because my goal is for you to develop a greater relationship with the Lord. You will need to read the scripture, think on the thought, pray the prayer, do the deed every day, and then journal what the Lord showed you for the day. If you can create a pattern for 30 days straight, then chances are you can Reset your life forever in Christ.

Day 1

Scripture of the day:

"But without faith it is impossible to please him: for he that cometh to God must believe that he is, and that he is a rewarder of them that diligently seek him." Hebrews 11:6

Thought of the day:

Whatever you feed will grow; whatever you starve will die.

Prayer of the day:

Lord, help me to pursue You with all my heart to close any gap in our relationship, so I can be more like You in my life.

Deed of the day:

Write down three scriptures on seeking God and meditate on them three different times today.

Journal of the day:

_____
_____
_____
_____

Day 2

Scripture of the day:

"And this is the confidence that we have in him, that, if we ask any thing according to his will, he heareth us:" 1 John 5:14

Thought of the day:

Prayer is designed to be a steering wheel not a spare tire.

Prayer of the day:

Give me a greater desire to share my life with You and communicate with You more.

Deed of the day:

Spend 15 minutes talking to God about what you need to change in your life and 15 minutes listening to what He has to say in response.

Journal of the day:

_____
_____
_____
_____
_____

Day 3

Scripture of the day:

"He that giveth unto the poor shall not lack: but he that hideth his eyes shall have many a curse." Proverbs 28:27

Thought of the day:

No one has ever become poor by giving to others.

Prayer of the day:

I rebuke a spirit of greed from my life in Jesus name. Lord, help me to be more generous in my giving to others and unto You.

Deed of the day:

Fast one meal today and give $3.00 to a missions group, church, or outreach organization.

Journal of the day:

_____
_____
_____
_____
_____

Day 4

Scripture of the day:

> *"Be sober, be vigilant; because your adversary the devil, as a roaring lion, walketh about, seeking whom he may devour:"* 1 Peter 5:8

Thought of the day:

> Always confront the Enemy! Never accommodate the enemy!

Prayer of the day:

> Lord, help me to be on the offensive today against the enemy. Instead of taking shots and catching darts thrown by the devil, allow me to score some points.

Deed of the day:

> Tell one person something good that Jesus has done for you recently in your life.

Journal of the day:

_____
_____
_____
_____

Day 5

Scripture of the day:

> *"Continue in prayer, and watch in the same with thanksgiving;"* Colossians 4:2

Thought of the day:

> Don't be spiritually M.I.A. or a spiritual streaker or you will become a spiritual P.O.W.

Prayer of the day:

> Lord, help me be alert to all the tricks, schemes, and traps of the enemy so I can be an overcomer.

Deed of the day:

> Literally put on the armor of God piece by piece by following the instruction in Ephesians 6:10-18.

Journal of the day:

_____
_____
_____
_____
_____
_____

Day 6

Scripture of the day:

"Let every thing that hath breath praise the Lord. Praise ye the Lord." Psalm 150:6

Thought of the day:

Praise contains the word raise. So, when I praise God, I get raised up.

Prayer of the day:

Lord, let praise to You be in my mind and come out of my mouth today in Jesus name.

Deed of the day:

Write down seven things that God does today that you can spend 15 minutes giving Him thanks for tonight before going to bed.

Journal of the day:

_____
_____
_____
_____
_____
_____

Day 7

Scripture of the day:

"Watch ye therefore, and pray always, that ye may be accounted worthy to escape all these things that shall come to pass, and to stand before the Son of man." Luke 21:36

Thought of the day:

By failing to prepare, you are preparing to fail.
— Benjamin Franklin

Prayer of the day:

Lord, help me to be prepared, not always get prepared. I want to be ready to fully obey you in all things.

Deed of the day:

Take 10 minutes to pray to the Lord while looking eastward, and just imagine what it will be like when Jesus returns for His church.

Journal of the day:

_____
_____
_____
_____

Day 8

Scripture of the day:

> *"Be not deceived; God is not mocked: for whatsoever a man soweth, that shall he also reap."* Galatians 6:7

Thought of the day:

> Whatever you sow is what you can expect to reap.

Prayer of the day:

> Lord, help me to do to others as I would have them do to me. I want to be a blessing.

Deed of the day:

> Find something nice to say to everyone you encounter throughout this day.

Journal of the day:

_____
_____
_____
_____
_____
_____

Day 9

Scripture of the day:

> *"Now faith is the substance of things hoped for, the evidence of things not seen."* Hebrews 11:1

Thought of the day:

> Hope is a prerequisite to faith. Don't let the enemy have either one.

Prayer of the day:

> Lord, increase my faith. I want to get your attention drawn to me by my faith in You.

Deed of the day:

> Read Hebrews 11 out loud to yourself three times today.

Journal of the day:

_____
_____
_____
_____
_____
_____
_____
_____

Day 10

Scripture of the day:

> *"But now ye also put off all these; anger, wrath, malice, blasphemy, filthy communication out of your mouth."* Colossians 3:8

Thought of the day:

Avoid evil like you avoid the plague.

Prayer of the day:

Lord, help me to guard my mind and watch my words.

Deed of the day:

Pay attention, and document bad thoughts, bad words, and bad actions. Pay $.25 for every bad thought, word, or action you indulge today. Give the total amount away as a special offering at your next church service.

Journal of the day:

_____
_____
_____
_____
_____

Day 11

Scripture of the day:

> *"Keep thy heart with all diligence; for out of it are the issues of life."* Proverbs 4:23

Thought of the day:

> The first job that God gave to mankind was to be a watchman.

Prayer of the day:

> Lord, help me to guard my eyes, ears, mind, and mouth from saying or doing anything displeasing to You.

Deed of the day:

> Only listen to Christian radio or watch Christian TV all day.

Journal of the day:

_____
_____
_____
_____
_____
_____

Day 12

Scripture of the day:

> *"So that from his body were brought unto the sick handkerchiefs or aprons, and the diseases departed from them, and the evil spirits went out of them."* Acts 19:12

Thought of the day:

Prayer cloths are points of contact with the anointing used to release the glory of the Lord.

Prayer of the day:

Lord, release Your anointing on the Earth, and let revival heal our land.

Deed of the day:

Give a prayer cloth to someone, and let them know you are praying for them.

Journal of the day:

_____
_____
_____
_____
_____
_____

Day 13

Scripture of the day:

"For if ye forgive men their trespasses, your heavenly Father will also forgive you: But if ye forgive not men their trespasses, neither will your Father forgive your trespasses." Matthew 6:14-15

Thought of the day:

When it comes to forgiveness it doesn't matter "Who is right"; it only matters "What is right."

Prayer of the day:

Lord, help me to choose to forgive others who have purposefully and intentionally done me wrong.

Deed of the day:

Make a call or write a letter to someone who hurt you and let them know you forgive them.

Journal of the day:

_____
_____
_____
_____

Day 14

Scripture of the day:

> *"There shall no evil befall thee, neither shall any plague come nigh thy dwelling."* Psalm 91:10

Thought of the day:

No weapon formed against me shall prosper.

Prayer of the day:

Lord, protect me from all attacks of the enemy. Let no weapon formed against me prosper.

Deed of the day:

Anoint every door, window, and room of your house with oil as you pray over them.

Journal of the day:

_____
_____
_____
_____
_____
_____
_____

Day 15

Scripture of the day:

> *"But ye shall receive power, after that the Holy Ghost is come upon you: and ye shall be witnesses unto me both in Jerusalem, and in all Judaea, and in Samaria, and unto the uttermost part of the earth."* Acts 1:8

Thought of the day:

> If you're ashamed of God now, He might be ashamed of you later.

Prayer of the day:

> Lord, help me to always be God-conscious, never self-conscious. Let me be a God-pleaser and not a man-pleaser.

Deed of the day:

> Look up a Christian poem on the internet and post it on social media websites.

Journal of the day:

_____
_____
_____
_____

Day 16

Scripture of the day:

"As cold waters to a thirsty soul, so is good news from a far country." Proverbs 25:25

Thought of the day:

Instead of looking for a blessing, go and be a blessing.

Prayer of the day:

Lord, help me to make somebody's day and make them glad that I'm alive.

Deed of the day:

Send an encouraging personal note in the mail, or through email, to three people today.

Journal of the day:

_____
_____
_____
_____
_____
_____
_____

Day 17

Scripture of the day:

"Behold, he that keepeth Israel shall neither slumber nor sleep." Psalm 121:4

Thought of the day:

Your body rests but your spirit never sleeps.

Prayer of the day:

Lord, help me to feed my spirit while my body rests, so I can wake up refreshed.

Deed of the day:

Shut off the radio and TV, and play the illustrated Bible while you sleep all night long.

Journal of the day:

_____
_____
_____
_____
_____
_____
_____
_____
_____

Day 18

Scripture of the day:

> *"Not as though I had already attained, either were already perfect: but I follow after, if that I may apprehend that for which also I am apprehended of Christ Jesus. Brethren, I count not myself to have apprehended: but this one thing I do, forgetting those things which are behind, and reaching forth unto those things which are before, I press toward the mark for the prize of the high calling of God in Christ Jesus."* Philippians 3:12-14

Thought of the day:

Take steps, not leaps, because Christianity is about progression, not perfection.

Prayer of the day:

Lord, help me to grow daily in my walk with You and never think more highly of myself than I should.

Deed of the day:

Go to a Celebrate Recovery Group or some recovery meeting tonight or this week.

Day 18-cont'd

Journal of the day:

Day 19

Scripture of the day:

> *"And the very God of peace sanctify you wholly; and I pray God your whole spirit and soul and body be preserved blameless unto the coming of our Lord Jesus Christ."*
> 1 Thessalonians 5:23

Thought of the day:

> You are not a body with a spirit but a spirit with a body.

Prayer of the day:

> Lord, help me to understand I am a threefold being created in Your likeness, and it's my responsibility to take care of myself.

Deed of the day:

> Get up 30 minutes early to exercise and pray before beginning your day.

Journal of the day:

_____
_____
_____
_____

Day 20

Scripture of the day:

"Beloved, think it not strange concerning the fiery trial which is to try you, as though some strange thing happened unto you: But rejoice, inasmuch as ye are partakers of Christ's sufferings; that, when his glory shall be revealed, ye may be glad also with exceeding joy." 1 Peter 4:12-13

Thought of the day:

Trials don't build character they reveal it.

Prayer of the day:

Lord, give me the strength to know that if You don't take me out of the fire, You will come in the fire with me.

Deed of the day:

Share your three favorite Christian songs with three people in your life.

Journal of the day:

_____
_____
_____

Day 21

Scripture of the day:

> *"Obey them that have the rule over you, and submit yourselves: for they watch for your souls, as they that must give account, that they may do it with joy, and not with grief: for that is unprofitable for you."* Hebrews 13:17

Thought of the day:

It's not your God-send's job to pursue you, but it's your job to pursue your God-send.

Prayer of the day:

Lord, bless my leaders, and help me to do a better job in making it easier on them to do their work.

Deed of the day:

Bless your headship today (Boss, parents, coach, spouse, pastor, etc.).

Journal of the day:

_____
_____
_____
_____

Day 22

Scripture of the day:

> *"Moreover when ye fast, be not, as the hypocrites, of a sad countenance: for they disfigure their faces, that they may appear unto men to fast. Verily I say unto you, They have their reward. But thou, when thou fastest, anoint thine head, and wash thy face; That thou appear not unto men to fast, but unto thy Father which is in secret: and thy Father, which seeth in secret, shall reward thee openly."* Matthew 6:16-18

Thought of the day:

Fasting is not a suggestion, it is a command.

Prayer of the day:

Lord, help me to deny my flesh, so I can say "no" to the devil and "yes" to You.

Deed of the day:

Fast lunch and listen to praise and worship music during lunchtime.

Day 22 – cont'd

Journal of the day:

Day 23

Scripture of the day:

> *"Many of them also which used curious arts brought their books together, and burned them before all men: and they counted the price of them, and found it fifty thousand pieces of silver. So mightily grew the word of God and prevailed."* Acts 19:19-20

Thought of the day:

> Get rid of things that represent evil before they end up getting rid of you.

Prayer of the day:

> Lord, give me discernment to know what is not beneficial to me serving You, and give me the courage to get rid of it.

Deed of the day:

> Go through your house, and get rid of every ungodly thing that doesn't please the Lord.

Journal of the day:

_____
_____
_____

Day 24

Scripture of the day:

> *"Behold, how good and how pleasant it is for brethren to dwell together in unity!"* Psalm 133:1

Thought of the day:

> The greatest threat to the church is not from without, but within. It's the disunity of the saints.

Prayer of the day:

> Lord, help me to walk in greater unity and understand oneness doesn't mean sameness.

Deed of the day:

> Think of three things you can do to make your church a better place.

Journal of the day:

_____
_____
_____
_____
_____

Day 25

Scripture of the day:

> *"Wisdom is the principal thing; therefore get wisdom: and with all thy getting get understanding."* Proverbs 4:7

Thought of the day:

> Wisdom is only an uncommon amount of common sense.

Prayer of the day:

> Lord, give me godly wisdom to discern the who, where, what, and why's of life.

Deed of the day:

> Read a chapter of a Christian book.

Journal of the day:

_____
_____
_____
_____
_____
_____
_____

Day 26

Scripture of the day:

> *"For I have received of the Lord that which also I delivered unto you, that the Lord Jesus the same night in which he was betrayed took bread: And when he had given thanks, he brake it, and said, Take, eat: this is my body, which is broken for you: this do in remembrance of me. After the same manner also he took the cup, when he had supped, saying, this cup is the new testament in my blood: this do ye, as oft as ye drink it, in remembrance of me. For as often as ye eat this bread, and drink this cup, ye do shew the Lord's death till he come."* 1 Corinthians 11:23-26

Thought of the day:

Communion brings a union that only God can give.

Prayer of the day:

Lord, let us always be thankful for what You have done for us and how You became the final sacrifice for mankind.

Day 26 – cont'd

Deed of the day:

> Take communion, either by yourself or as a family, tonight before going to bed. Follow the instructions from 1 Corinthians 11.

Journal of the day:

Day 27

Scripture of the day:

"And now abideth faith, hope, charity, these three; but the greatest of these is charity." 1 Corinthians 13:13

Thought of the day:

Without love, we are nothing.

Prayer of the day:

Lord, help me to love like You love.

Deed of the day:

Bring donuts, or snacks, to work to bless those in your office.

Journal of the day:

_____
_____
_____
_____
_____
_____
_____
_____

Day 28

Scripture of the day:

> *"And they overcame him by the blood of the Lamb, and by the word of their testimony; and they loved not their lives unto the death."* Revelation 12:11

Thought of the day:

> We go through tests, so God can give us a testimony.

Prayer of the day:

> Lord, give me the courage to share the good news of Christ with others.

Deed of the day:

> Write down your testimony on paper.

Journal of the day:

_____
_____
_____
_____
_____
_____
_____

Day 29

Scripture of the day:

> *"Give, and it shall be given unto you; good measure, pressed down, and shaken together, and running over, shall men give into your bosom. For with the same measure that ye mete withal it shall be measured to you again."* Luke 6:38

Thought of the day:

Abundant living is abundant giving.

Prayer of the day:

Lord, make me a giver and not a taker.

Deed of the day:

Give three people a gospel tract, and invite them to church.

Journal of the day:

_____
_____
_____
_____
_____
_____

Day 30

Scripture of the day:

"A man that hath friends must shew himself friendly: and there is a friend that sticketh closer than a brother." Proverbs 18:24

Thought of the day:

A friend comes in when everyone else goes out.

Prayer of the day:

Lord, help me to be the friend to others that I am looking for myself.

Deed of the day:

Introduce yourself to three new people today.

Journal of the day:

Chapter 8

RESET Scriptures

"I beseech you therefore, brethren, by the mercies of God, that ye present your bodies a living sacrifice, holy, acceptable unto God, which is your reasonable service. And be not conformed to this world: but be ye transformed by the renewing of your mind, that ye may prove what is that good, and acceptable, and perfect, will of God." Romans 12:1-2

"I will open rivers in high places, and fountains in the midst of the valleys: I will make the wilderness a pool of water, and the dry land springs of water." Isaiah 41:18

"Be careful for nothing; but in every thing by prayer and supplication with thanksgiving let your requests be made known unto God. And the peace of God, which passeth all

understanding, shall keep your hearts and minds through Christ Jesus. Finally, brethren, whatsoever things are true, whatsoever things are honest, whatsoever things are just, whatsoever things are pure, whatsoever things are lovely, whatsoever things are of good report; if there be any virtue, and if there be any praise, think on these things." Philippians 4:6-8

"It is of the LORD's mercies that we are not consumed, because his compassions fail not. They are new every morning: great is thy faithfulness." Lamentations 3:22-23

"For which cause we faint not; but though our outward man perish, yet the inward man is renewed day by day. For our light affliction, which is but for a moment, worketh for us a far more exceeding and eternal weight of glory; While we look not at the things which are seen, but at the things which are not seen: for the things which are seen are temporal; but the

things which are not seen are eternal."
2 Corinthians 4:16-18

"Brethren, I count not myself to have apprehended: but this one thing I do, forgetting those things which are behind, and reaching forth unto those things which are before," Philippians 3:13

"Repent ye therefore, and be converted, that your sins may be blotted out, when the times of refreshing shall come from the presence of the Lord." Acts 3:19

"Bless the LORD, O my soul: and all that is within me, bless his holy name. Bless the LORD, O my soul, and forget not all his benefits: Who forgiveth all thine iniquities; who healeth all thy diseases; Who redeemeth thy life from destruction; who crowneth thee with lovingkindness and tender mercies; Who satisfieth thy mouth with good things; so that

thy youth is renewed like the eagle's." Psalm 103:1-5

"And he that sat upon the throne said, Behold, I make all things new. And he said unto me, Write: for these words are true and faithful." Revelation 21:5

"And he spake also a parable unto them; No man putteth a piece of a new garment upon an old; if otherwise, then both the new maketh a rent, and the piece that was taken out of the new agreeth not with the old. And no man putteth new wine into old bottles; else the new wine will burst the bottles, and be spilled, and the bottles shall perish. But new wine must be put into new bottles; and both are preserved." Luke 5:36-38

"Remember ye not the former things, neither consider the things of old. Behold, I will do a

---

new thing; now it shall spring forth; shall ye not know it? I will even make a way in the wilderness, and rivers in the desert." Isaiah 43:18-19

"Therefore if any man be in Christ, he is a new creature: old things are passed away; behold, all things are become new." 2 Corinthians 5:17

"Though thy beginning was small, yet thy latter end should greatly increase." Job 8:7

"And I will restore to you the years that the locust hath eaten, the cankerworm, and the caterpillar, and the palmerworm, my great army which I sent among you." Joel 2:25

"Therefore we are buried with him by baptism into death: that like as Christ was raised up from the dead by the glory of the Father, even

---

so we also should walk in newness of life."
Romans 6:4

"Create in me a clean heart, O God; and renew a right spirit within me." Psalm 51:10

"And be renewed in the spirit of your mind;" Ephesians 4:23

"Wherefore I put thee in remembrance that thou stir up the gift of God, which is in thee by the putting on of my hands." 2 Timothy 1:6

"For I know the thoughts that I think toward you, saith the LORD, thoughts of peace, and not of evil, to give you an expected end." Jeremiah 29:11

Conclusion

This book is really all about the Reset. The pages of this book provide the tools necessary to define if there is a need for Reset, and the wisdom to give you direction to get from where you are at to where God wants you to be. Resetting is about the rebooting, reinventing, and restoring.

> Reboot = to shut down in order to restart; to start anew.

> Reinvent = to make major changes to improve the condition of something.

> Restore = to return something to its original condition.

Those words defined explain the entire purpose of this book. It is my prayer, and God's will, for us to shut some things down in order to start anew. We can't keep doing the same things in life and expect a different result. Major changes need to be made, so

we can improve ourselves to be productive people for Christ in the Kingdom of God.

If you want to make a difference in this world, there must first be a difference that takes place in your own personal heart. The ultimate goal of Resetting is for the Lord to return you back to the original position and condition you were at before you got off course, and to thrust you forward into fulfilling your destiny. Your cooperation with God in this Resetting process is essential in ensuring that you reach the highest level of success and satisfaction in life.

www.ingramcontent.com/pod-product-compliance
Lightning Source LLC
Chambersburg PA
CBHW031427290426
44110CB00011B/557